CW00456723

Copyright © Trevor Conway 2023

ISBN 9781731036865

Acknowledgements

Some of these poems first appeared in the following publications: *New Contrast* (South Africa), *Dreich* (UK), *The Lake* (UK), *The Galway Review* (Ireland), *Squawk Back* (USA), *Artistic Atlas of Galway* (Ireland), *StepAway* (UK), *Allegro Poetry Magazine* (UK) and *Cerasus Magazine* (UK).

Many thanks to all those who gave feedback on the poems in this book through writing groups, classes and general chat. In particular, thanks to the following: Sandra Coffey, Jimi McDonnell, Jenny Hall, Sarah Clancy, Aoibheann McCann, Malgosia Doczyk, Liza Bolton and Kevin Higgins.

Thank you to all who contributed to funding this book. Your help means a lot.

As ever, to my family, thank you for the fun, advice, love and support.

for Sandra and Nicole

Author's Note

Two major forces shaped this collection. The first was becoming a father, navigating the uneven, shifting terrain of raising a child. The second force, though less strong, was the global coronavirus pandemic, which directed my focus inward, to the home. In the midst of all the sadness, anxiety and frustration at being confined and unable to see family or friends, I thought it was important to celebrate the space in which we live. I was also interested in describing the sheer enormity of effort behind all aspects of the home, the physical, mental and emotional work involved.

It's not as if the theme of home hasn't been explored in poetry before. It's a fairly common theme in writing anthologies, for example. So, why another book centred around the home? Well, I suppose you could say the same about any theme that's been done before. Why write about love or death, nature or war? The short response: because my perspective is different. Everyone's is. That's justification enough, I think, but I also wanted to steer clear of blandness and offer something new.

Hence, I sought creative ways to burrow into the topic of home. I wanted to focus, at times, on aspects that others might have ignored, that the reader might not expect. For example, I've threaded this book with poems written from the perspective of various rooms in a house. Each has its own character, its own tone and views on the inhabitants, and on how they interact with the space around them. I've also pursued more familiar ideas centred around the home, such as poems capturing the experience of household tasks like doing the laundry ("Cycles"), cleaning a room ("Saturday"), cooking ("Cottage Pie"), washing dishes ("Residue") and removing ashes from a fire ("Clearing"). I've worked on these relentlessly – or "scrubbed" them, you could say – to give them some original spirit. And if I'm honest, I tried my best to avoid what you might call sub-par imitations of Heaney.

In dealing with the home, it seemed to me that there were two main pillars to consider: home as a physical structure and home as a concept. I've given examples of the former above. As regards the concept of home, this is where my leaning towards more philosophical poetry came into play. Philosophical poems were dominant in my early writing, less so in the last ten years, but a few of these poems qualify. In "Migrant", I consider the forces of town and country in my life, both of them shaping my sense of home. "A Sligo Rhyme" takes a simpler approach to my relationship with my hometown. "Terra Firma", meanwhile, addresses the idea of owning property. (Comparisons with certain communist principles are probably unavoidable here, but it wasn't my intention to echo such principles, only to consider the proposition of a world without the ownership of land.)

Ireland has always been my home in a conceptual sense. That won't change, even with a physical change of space. Growing up in Sligo, with its varied natural features, certainly gave me an appreciation for nature and the countryside. This appreciation was more evident in my early writing, but some of it survives here. The dominance of Yeats in Sligo's cultural life surely influenced me too. His words are in the public consciousness there, and there was plenty of feeding in them to nourish and excite me as a young writer. Later, Galway fostered my writing in a different way. As a city, it felt like a home for writers, artists, students and the like. The semi-feckless gathered together and made something serious of their art. I felt I belonged there, and it gave me an affinity for city life which I hadn't previously had. But after fourteen years, other notions came into play. Mediterranean ones, to be specific.

During the writing of this collection, I moved with my wife and daughter to Tarragona, an hour or so south of Barcelona. Some of the locals think of it as Spain. Others call it Catalunya. (I can never get used to calling it the English equivalent, "Catalonia", for some reason.) Among these people, the concept of their nationhood differs. I often think it must be like Ireland a hundred years ago, when some people wanted independence and others preferred to stay with Britain. Of course, such differing views of nationhood are still strong in the north of Ireland,

and I suspect the situation there promotes a certain kind of restlessness that I can't imagine. I sometimes wonder if such restlessness is helpful or detrimental to a writer, but that's another discussion for another book.

I suppose parenthood, too, can be thought of as a concept. It comes with theories and approaches, ideas of what's right or wrong. It feels like much more than a concept, though, when you're woken in the middle of the night, trying to get your daughter back to sleep. It's my hope that I've given a fairly balanced reflection of parenthood (or at least my experience of it) in this book. I was conscious of the need to avoid an overdose of sentiment. It was difficult to find ways into poems that essentially celebrated my daughter, or my relationship with her. There was a constant questioning: is this worthy of a poem for someone else to read? Is it original? Interesting? Or is it ultimately self-referential drivel? A few pieces didn't make it past the cull for these reasons.

In detailing the more difficult aspects of parenthood, I was wary of wallowing in self-pity. That said, the daily frustrations of parenthood might seem small in theory or when taken individually, but I think every parent has moments or periods of emotional struggle. At least you can prepare yourself to some degree for those frustrations. What was more of a shock for me were the effects of sleep deprivation caused by repeated night-time wakings over a period of a few months. I found it to be one of the most traumatic things I've experienced. Its emotional consequences were complicated and surprisingly long-lasting (staying with me well after the relevant period of sleep problems had ended).

Perhaps the most unexpected consequence was its effect on my creativity. It wasn't that I couldn't write, more that I didn't enjoy writing, and I didn't rate anything I was writing over a period of about a year. Up until then, since I'd started writing, aged fifteen or so, I'd become used to giddy excitement with a pen and paper to hand. This was a daily experience for me. Words and phrases were enchanting things. Poems and stories were little worlds unto themselves, and I was an avid traveller among them. After twenty-five years of such a relationship with writing, I'd lost that passion. And I wasn't sure I'd ever get it back.

I also weighed the value of my writing in a more practical sense, in terms of money and the time spent on writing when I could have been with my daughter. I lost sight of the value it held for me on a personal level. This was a mistake. I guess it's true to say that when artists – when *people* – focus too much on measuring the hours spent on something against some idea of a financial or practical benefit, they tend to lose something of themselves. I'd appeal to anyone who questions their passion for such reasons to remember when they were younger and first in love with that thing. Passion will return. It took time, but I found my love for poetry again. This collection is a testament to that.

Contents

Foundation

Orientation

Bearing

Insulation

Decay

14

Foundation

Labour

I saw green till diggers came
and clawed it all away,
soil and stone revealed,
cement swept in thick currents.
Heavy pipes were hoisted down,
and stubborn slabs sandwiched all
to a subterranean fate.

Walls rose from cinder blocks.
A second floor flourished
with a deluge of timber,
and slanted tiles clung to wood,
shiny as reptile skin.
Men threaded wire through holes,
upholstering walls with electric current,
while others laboured on plain frescoes
of white plaster.

Garden soil was ruffled, rolled,
raked and seeded, raked again.
Vans arrived, disgorging beds,
things cocooned in sleek plastic,
wardrobes, tables, a well-fed couch.

And one day, when all seemed quiet,
car doors flung open.
Children spewed
with quick steps and spiky cries
that coloured the dying afternoon.
Curious neighbours emerged at windows,

reliving a time
when their gardens were yet to green.

Cycles

She sniffs fabric
for the faint, sour scent of sweat,
determines the chosen
and shrugs them off hangers,
pressing under her arm
a mass that twists and hardens
to a lump like gathered dough.

And as the slow beast grunts to its labour,
she imagines thick conditioner
working a kind of massage
on cotton, linen,
wool and denim.
Foam blizzards its manic churning
until she returns to the rumble
that spins all colour to soup.

Wet and ashamed, it seems to her,
the heavy haul is pulled from the belly,
delivered from hand to basket
rich with the smell of detergent.
Their arms stretched to the pinch of a peg,
garments offer their weight to the sky,
and sudden gusts
synchronise their dance.

The hours that bring on night
leave her pegs empty as moths wrapped in silk.
Only when preparing for bed
can she raise each garment from the basket:

folding clothes away in a drawer
is too much like a burial.

Ongoing

A Galway winter
sings its own lament outside.
In this bar of students and hospital workers,
families of patients with worried faces,
we inhabit a quiet corner,
where you wince to the tune of your pain,
your hand like a plaster across your belly.

We've come from a clinical room
littered with leaflets and their gaudy phrases:
"what is miscarriage?",
"coping with your loss".
It all seems premature,
as the nurse couldn't label your hurt,
speaking of how the signs suggested
our child was "not ongoing".

I have no practice
in these situations,
can only speak of easing your pain,
of trying again
– after a tactful period –
already consigning our child to the past.

Soon,
a doctor with a gentler hand
will reveal all your discomfort
as a child announcing its presence
like a drunken guest
stumbling into the furniture of a new environment.

We'll give her names
– Nicole, Veruna –
the latter sutured from both our mothers.
And a year from now,
all our pensive inertia will seem like potential energy
sprung into kinetic form
– night-feeds, nappies, buttoning vests –
as we dote on milk-morphined eyes.

We'll watch her together
as she takes a step,
and smile to each other
as she keeps on going.

Fourteen Months of Photos

To think of how your inky eyes
unclouded to allow confessions of light,
how recent months
have thinned your face,
your timid chin striking out on its own.

These pictures whisper, "See how she's grown,"
"see how emotion has kneaded her cheeks",
and all those curls we coveted
finally made their unruly tribute
to your weary mother,
offering their sparks to a Sligo wind.

But no photo can speak of hope
or sleep-shy nights,
your mother's Alpine blood
or a hurried decision
to birth you by blade.
They're images we hold within,
as firm as the instinct that placed your finger into your
    mouth
when I first held your warmth and your weight.

Other images we have yet to see:
a schoolbag tight like a barnacle to your back,
the jagged, crayon scrawl of your name,
your face womaned in make-up.

And there'll be a day
when you seek pictures of us.

You'll laugh at our antique clothes
and find ideals in our faces,
but you can never know the past
your mother and I shared
before you stirred our present.

Cottage Pie

It begins with Rooster potatoes,
like many an Irish meal,
pealed so quick slender skins
stick to the sink like baby fish.

Cut, cube, consign to steam,
and while your beef stock wafts
through a bowl of boiled water,
cut your carrot round, and fry
till it shines like a coin freshly minted.

Now,
you're ready
for the minced beef.
Rouse it like a jostling crowd
till all its red heads are dulled,
assuming the hue of a rainy cloud.

Onions are odd,
have you noticed?
They come clothed, expecting winter,
but you must disrobe yours,
dice
and scatter.

Now, concentrate on tomato purée:
squirt it like a bad signature,
pursued by strokes of Worcestershire sauce,
some careful dabs of salt.
Add the stock, and it will simmer

from soggy ground to firmer soil.

By now, your potatoes are soft and sweaty –
a state you'll enhance with milk and butter.
Use the masher to curl it all
onto the waiting meat.
A few minutes in the oven
will fix your potato to a sepia crown.

Present it to all,
but as you place it under chin,
remember not to misname it:
shepherds mind sheep; they cook with lamb,
not beef.
This is a pie fit for a cottage
and all who gather to share a piece.

Shelf Life

There is a pageant
of fascinated souls here,
aisles piled with products
vivid as paintings on gallery walls.
One waits by the door,
fixing his hood, a hostage of rain
that batters an afternoon beat on the roof.

A man with a thin moustache
gropes loaves of sliced pan
till he finds one that yields most
to the curl of his cracked hand.
An old lady with a trolley
squeaking and jerking with neglect
eyes jars on a high shelf,
jammed tight as stained glass.

There is relief in the breath of the freezer,
its chicken corpses dismembered, minced,
mummified in frosted breadcrumb.

Time to consult the shopping list,
be sure nothing's missed.
Time to study the casts of queues
and make a decision.

A man with mountainous arms,
red meat pressed to his chest,
regrets his choice as the cashier dashes
away from her till on some daft errand.

He closes his eyes and wonders
how much of his life he'll spend in queues,
how many minutes and hours
waiting,
regretting,
as others fumble
with petty change.

October

First oil truck of winter
through the sleepy housing estate,
and with its tired rumble,
pale faces emerge at dark windows.

Chimneys offer
a broadcast of smoke
from those who've already lit fires
as breezes sent from Siberia
rattle raindrops on bony branches.

And that hum you hear
isn't the company of a dying wasp;
it's the hum of a boiler
pumping warmth
to the many corners of a home.

A Sligo Rhyme

It isn't quite fashionable now
to write nostalgic poems of home
wearing their sentiment heavy and long.

Some scribbles are meant for drawers,
stuffed away like ragged shirts,
as public taste gallops on.

But there's a seam of Sligo within me,
and if I was to undo myself,
I'd write of Rosses Point
thrusting its nose toward the Atlantic
above a fortune of waves
bright as shuffling coin.

Benbulben might be a dozing shepherd
above the flocks of Drumcliffe,
and all the trees of Hazelwood
deer in autumn fur,
their barky antlers gathered round
Lough Gill's sleepy water.

Such a wistful poem
might console me for all the distance and time
I've pushed between myself and home.

One day, I hope to find
a way to wear the years so light
I'll stitch a Sligo rhyme.

Hallway

Welcome!

Step inside.

But please, first, wipe your feet.

Feel free to explore,
to examine details and speculate
if you can't tell mahogany from oak.

You might even want to admire
the small sculpture your host created
one aimless year in Italy.

Ask her – she'll tell you all about it.

I know these people –
these good parents, these busy children.
I know the signature of their steps,
each with its own rhythm and weight.

See how I lift these jagged stairs
like a ballerina held at the hips?

Sometimes, I admit, I feel used,
like a train station –
never the end of anyone's journey.

But enough of that!

I see them often,
if not for long.

At least I'm not the attic.

Saturday

Some know the rattle of grit
up a hoover's metal shaft
– a sound like children playing –
till one hand gauges suction,
gloving a tune against the palm.

They run a cloth
along the curves of skirting boards,
alert to how sunlight fixes
dust like a thin tide
on dark surfaces.

A rubbed bulb can draw a quiver,
and at that heady height,
the thickness of grime on a curtain rail
can shock them into action,
stepping on chairs to gather its blackness.

They may choose the brush
to herd dirt into corners,
sending its shaft under structures
like a piston, probing.
Others prefer the choreography of furniture.

When water bleeds from a mop,
devoured whole in a bucket's jaws,
they watch strands of steam rise
like the tendrils of a jellyfish,
and bleach, to them, smells like perfume.

Orientation

Clearing

You bow to a ruin of ash,
shovel in hand,
discrete as an archaeologist so as not to rouse it,
knowing that even in an airless room,
loosened ash can make itself
slight as a vulture
asleep on a thermal.

The angle you keep
as you skim your cargo into the bucket
cannot be sacrificed,
so you tilt its metal mouth,
though it will press its dust like pollen
along the channels of your fingertips.

You send the brush sniffing corners
till curls of beige unsettle and swirl
like liquid tails through the air.
This cracked concrete
houses little histories of dust
that might not be discovered for years.

The final, prehistoric grunt of steel
tightens your muscles to a wince;
and yes, it's strange to call it a shovel
when shoving is an act to avoid.

Native Tongue

Carrer d'Orosi, Tarragona

I speak to Spaniards
who sand away the ends of their words
as if to fit them together.
I can't understand a thing.
"*Perdona,*" I say, "*no rápido para mí*",
and as I speak, they wait, amused,
my clumsy tongue slow as a saw
looting their language at random.

"Goggin, goggin, dahs, goh,
degud, degud,"
my two-year-old interrupts.
She's scraping at words too,
maybe even offering tips
on how to parent her better.

In time, she and I will speak the same language
and pluck from our throats
feathery words to fly
through fairy tales and school books,
explanations and arguments,
occasional
emotional
crises.

There'll be moody silence,
but she might someday pierce a moment
between the cries of her own child

to tell me how good a dad I've been
or – as she'll be almost a native
in this land of toasted skin –
to mend my mangled Spanish.

Stopping for Death

I was five when my brother explained
old age and the concept of death.
No sooner did I hear the words
than I lamented –
for my parents, not myself.

Unable to fathom an orphan life,
I resolved to follow
whenever the day arrived
that their bodies were seasoned with soil.

I dreamt of blood and blade, a rope
bent softly to a noose.
Often, I stared at telephone wires,
supposing it took one touch
to die, eavesdropping
on adult talk.

And yet, the birds chirped happily there.
They even seemed to charge their songs
from the hidden sparks of its current.

As body and mind ripened,
my childish vow withered.
Over the years, my parents aged
like dinner plates, chipped and stained,
and all my morbid fears
were nourished by a new life
I had to guard from danger.

She plays with toys,
tending to all their cries and tears,
their plastic lives born in death.
I'll teach her of darker things,
hoping she'll survive
to find me, one day,
quiet as a doll asleep in bed.

New-born

4am: craving rest,
your aching arm could wither soon,
rocking a child you half regret,
unable to hold this tune.
You're losing time, leaking sense,
on speaking terms with the moon,
but somehow,
this night will pass.

You think it shouldn't be so hard,
though you find a kind of fuel
in smiles and cries, thickening hair,
when molten emotions cool.
You've wounded those close to you,
shocked that you've been so cruel,
but tomorrow, there's time
to mend your words.

This night might break you.
Days undone will do it too.
Sometimes, your belief and courage
will sink under murky moods,
but you'll find yourself in the clearing
with a child who sees the world anew.
And one day,
you will too.

No Small Thing

I saw men who were fitter fathers than I could ever be.
For years, they prowled the breadth of my vision,
gladly pouring their will and energy
down the throats of slender faces smiling up at them.
Though children were small,
I saw how they gorged
on your time and your spirit,
till you sacrificed your self,
which seemed
to me
no small thing.

Something bred within me which thinned my fear,
as if the ground around me changed,
and with it, my weight.
I sensed the smallness of time ahead,
could smell parenthood reeking from my peers.
And suddenly,
one cold October morning,
I imagined you into being.

Within a year,
your mother gave you to the light.
You were small as my doubts,
and you snuffed them out
the moment I held you,
watching your finger
enter the black pupil of your mouth.
And you,
my child,

were no small thing.

Baby Steps

She is a creature coming to terms
with the new physics
of her bony machinery,

moving
        along
                by careful
                        degrees.

Hands pressed to the wall,
she reads the room like a text,

punctuated by gaps   and prospects.

She learns to explore
her wordless universe of shape and texture,
engaging with the science of dirty corners,
and so the work of watching her grows.

Probing possibility, to her,
is a serious occupation
as she clutches chairs and tables,
learning the laws of limitation.

Her mastery is quiet,
her thought like a snake slithering ahead.

One leg lifts.

And when she looks to her mother,

I fear
      that walking
            is imminent.

Oh, Man

As if their world is made of glass,
some men step with bleeding toes.
Just imagine
how they cope
with feeling they might be men at last.

The cries they hear
come from voices yet to tussle with words,
and though they dream of being redeemed with the flow
    of milk
and nappies full as the shell of a snail,
sometimes, they sour
to doubts and moods they can never reason
to the edge of their minds
like bedtime monsters.

Tell them they have loved well
if you ever see them stumble,
as they will need to walk again
before they can teach another.

And then,
having taught,
they are porcelain.

Kitchen

God, I'm tired.

Maybe it's the fluorescent light,
the boiling,
the sizzling,
the bland rigmarole of staining and cleaning,
windows sweating,
drawers yawning,
the saucepans' tinny clamour.

Even when I reek of bleach,
I know there's mugs, crumbs
neglected in a whirl of plans,
giddy chat of the beach.

Conversation
comes in fragments
between blizzards of chopping and stirring,
the awkward dance
of those in the way,
bodies always turning.

Then, there's moments
quiet as a widow before a grave:

Someone sits with coffee,
stares out the window
with eyes that follow the flight of a bird
or a thick branch
nodding in agreement with the wind.

That's when I sometimes think
it might be worth it, after all.

PVC

I remember when wood
was suddenly not good enough.
One neighbour abandoned it,
and soon, another;
three more conspired in the same month,
their windows like pristine pools
that seemed to scorn all rot.

The men who came to our home
bartered easily with complication.
They did their work and moved on,
left us marvelling at noise reduction,
watching traffic from the kitchen table
like our own silent film.

Between the layers of double glazing,
my boyish mind imagined
an insect trapped for eternity
like a specimen in a museum.
In time, all that was trapped was moisture,
forming cataracts on our vision.

We hardly noticed,
as we could see what needed to be seen,
and we never thought that what was new
was no better than what came before.

Bearing

Residue

When stomachs are busy tending
to the newly arrived by fork and knife,
suds germinate from green sludge
squirted from a wheezing bottle.
Soon, it will evolve
to a billowing creature of busy cells.

Into its belly, you shove a rabble
of plastic, steel and ceramic.
The clatter and scrape of empty plates echoes through
    the house
as warm water persuades your hands
to blush, as if embarrassed
at all these smears and rags of food.

Each of your pans, dishes and pots,
one day, will seem to you,
in a rare kitchen epiphany,
beyond the tasks you ask of it.
And you will plan
a trip to the shop.

Despite your frantic shuffling of cutlery,
when you have lifted the plug and admired
plates, glasses and bowls
set to dry like a gleaming city,
the last suds will retreat,
persuaded away like dandelion seeds,
to reveal a knife
smudged in butter.

49

Attic

No-one comes to visit,
so how can I not wonder
what it is they find so repulsive?

- My dark breath?
- The vast clutter?
- The fact that I lack the common need
  to clog the world with noise?

I could solicit attention,
sending mysterious sounds
down to their beds at night,
faint at first,
then somewhat certain.
In time, enough to wake them.

~~But I was never so inclined.~~

Such company they pair me with:
battered boxes, crippled chairs,
Christmas trees strangled in lights,
a dead man's clothes, video cassettes,
a one-string violin.

What?
Did you say something?
Sometimes, I hear things.
I'm sure they can't be real.

Perhaps they find me odd,

like an alcoholic aunt who's come to stay
for an undefined period.

But how could I not be,
when they put such odd things into me?

Migrant

I began where the breeze was clean,
reared on fields and streams
till town offered a torrent of comforts,

all things huddled,
desires fed
by the tap of sole on concrete.

Still, I was drawn to grass, leeching
in slices of park and lawn
or spread out blatant as football pitches,

reminding me that towns were fields
till people came, deposited lives,
noise and tension,
hard ambitions.

In time, I found what I was
in trees cut to the shape of benches,
pigeons gurgling the same old tune.

Country trickled through my thoughts,
dropped its silt
on streets and walls,

and after a while,
I barely heard the noise:
it became another stream.

Forwarding

Having found a new home that fits his frilly criteria,
he opens the kitchen press
which housed his food for three years.
Consulting its contents,
he scripts his final meals accordingly,
conceiving of waste as a minimalist art.

And with less room for books
in the new space he'll inhabit,
he must reach a decision
on whether he'll ever read
the conjugations of five hundred Spanish verbs.

Despite his careful preparations,
he hasn't yet considered
the reservoir of spirit he'll need to drain,
scrubbing and mopping from room to room,
in the final hours before departure.

A feeling will flourish
– exhilaration, with a dash of despair –
snagging his mind on memories,
whispering, "The past is a thing to be mourned."

When he can clean no more,
he'll gather his bags, stand at the door
and think of the sprinkling of Spanish he's learned:
they use *estar*, not *ser*,
when speaking of someone's address,
the verb "to be" as a temporary thing,

as if to say
all homes
are fleeting.

After the Pandemic

Those who survived – and there were many –
waded deep into plans,
having emerged from homely hibernation
with the veiny traces of face masks
printed about their ears.

They still were inclined
to keep their distance
as they watched the cranes swing back into life
and heard the drills, the chisels and hammers
cackling through the morning.

Thieves lamented,
unable to approach
without arousing suspicion,
and everyone hoped the next pandemic
would be a problem
endured by some aloof generation.

In quieter moments,
when freedom had the scent of normality again
and homes allowed sovereign thoughts,
some reflected on those
who hadn't survived
to see the world begin again.

Hazelwood Pitch

The studs of boots have churned the dirt
for years below this grass,
a million cups of shadow
stamped in a Calry season.

Some could be mine,
though two decades have passed
since I endured the sky's moods
with blue and yellow tight to my back.

There, I rose like a wave in the wind,
plucked the ball from the air,
turned sharp, lost my marker,
lashed it to the net.

On the twenty-one, I fumbled,
gave the ball away.
The opposition sent it high
between our shivering posts.

Here, I gave an awful pass.
In the box, I blocked a goal,
fell to the pain of a sprained foot
a few yards from there.

And once, near the forty-five,
without the scent of a thought,
I launched it crudely to the air,
scored the winning point.

Rooneys, Kellys, Devaneys, Flynns,
brothers, cousins, schoolmates played.
Hugh McLoughlin called our names
in a voice that boomed across the pitch.

Now, my shoes make no impression
as I walk across the grass,
but sweat returns when I look at the posts
and find they're in my range.

Bathroom

I see you look in the mirror:
twelves times a minute,
maybe more.

All you visitors ask for me.
You don't care
that I aspire to be bright and sleek.
You ruffle the mat over cold tile
until it rises like ploughed soil.
You smudge my sink with make-up and grime.

I am devoted to the body, whole,
and if I seem harsh,
you might return by evening
to avail of more forgiving light.

I harbour rain, rivers and lakes,
whatever's required to cleanse you.
And I echo. Oh, how I echo!

But can you imagine the smells I endure:
mint, lavender, potpourri,
vanilla and much, much more.

Always remember, I've seen you
unwinding soft paper,
staring at the towel that hangs like a bat,
and all that follows.

Biscuits

Have you ever pondered the ubiquity,
the sheer endurance,
of the household biscuit,
in all its brisk forms and textures:
the bourbon and rich tea,
the Spanish tan of the ginger nut,
the albino custard cream,
digestives and oat-proud hobnobs,
the fig roll's aspiration to a meal?

Study the art of dipping.
A biscuit welcomes tea like a brother,
warps to its weight,
but it will droop
as if on the point of sleep,
and if you are too ambitious,
it may collapse like a dusty wall.

Cookies came,
with complications of fruit and chocolate chip,
and so, you might think, extinction loomed.
The biscuit survived,
cherished by hosts
and stomachy visitors.

Despite all this, it might be wise
to keep your cupboard empty
if you are the kind
who finds the daily presence of the biscuit
just too much

provocation.

Spare Socks

I often wonder
where they go
as I creep about with glacial toes.
Between the wash
and when I dress,
there's some mysterious process:
each load yields less and less.

They could be snug
on a stranger's feet,
slumped at the door of a dark street.
Those I draw
from the pile with care
will never again become a pair:
they even seem to droop in despair.

I recently found
a telling clue
during a romantic rendezvous:

I noticed my girlfriend
sniffing my shirt.
She even wore it next day to work.

In her home,
I picture a box
full of all my errant socks,

so maybe tonight,
I'll ask politely,

"Honey, do you know where my socks might be?"

Men at Work

She will watch a saw thrust and retreat,
sure as a snake bite,
repeating its noisy endeavour,
and, as sawdust drizzles to the floor by her little feet,
she'll reach out a finger.

When a nail disappears into timber
under the force of three measured strikes,
she will smile,
looking at its head, level with wood,
as if she knows this is what a nail most likes.

She listens for hours
to saw-sigh and timber-fall,
the nervous rambling of an old drill,
tuned anew to how the world is made –
by silent men with God-like powers
and tools like toys bent to a stubborn will.

But does she know that women, too, can do such things?
And will she learn by observation
that men can excel at cleaning and baking,
the rehabilitation of dirty clothes,
that anyone's pen is for writing?

She sees that work is an art,
but she'll learn that art is work too.
When I sit at the desk to make my start,
she sets me the task of slicing bread;
I watch the crumb-fall as she chews.

Insulation

Careful

Familiar things were predators
once our child flexed her feet.
Our eyes became greedy
for information of the ahead,
what might emerge from streets and doorways,
drivers in love with their phones.

Staircases were sharpened teeth,
and pools of water
had a stomach for bones and breath.
Our own balcony, even, betrayed us
with gaps that seemed too generous,
so we fenced our fear with the sides of cots
strung against it, rigid as ribs.

We spoke of danger
before it stalked our daughter,
and so we did these things
to make her terrain soft as a tongue,
but we never foresaw the need
for fences around our thoughts.

These were stronger,
encased both our minds
and huddled us together
to protect us from sadness and anger,
moods that gave us claws to wound
when we had bodies starved of sleep,
emotions we could barely fathom.

Generation Procreation

They breed on social media:
photos of pink skin wrapped burrito-tight
in soft, cotton blankets,
swollen wrinkles for eyes –
another man I knew as a boy
huddled over a Summerhill desk
has finally surrendered to parenthood.

A cold contagion has taken root
among my peers, all our eyes
fixed on a vast horizon:
death and birth are serious things
after forty years of life.

Some of these men
fathered by default,
others by accident or assumption,
and some, I imagine, through sheer boredom.
A few, too – I see it in their faces –
gave into a brand of fear.

In forty years, they'll flood again,
these wincing creatures – our grandchildren,
with all the bald glory of their being;
or there'll be photos of us,
posted by our own children
to announce that we will be no more,
to silently say
death is contagious too.

Daughter's Gift

Laid on the bed, towel beneath her,
nappy, wipes, tissue, powder
set to the side like a surgeon's tools,
I unbutton her warm sleepsuit
(just as the surgeon unbuttoned her mother).

I separate the nappy from her hips,
immune now to these smells.
With one hand, I hoist her legs
as she wriggles like that part of me
which swam the canals of her mother.

A moment of stillness
before the shallow baptism of a wet wipe.
I swab away the mess
to reveal the nappy's red imprint
like a hot fossil on her skin.

She once expected rash strokes,
raising herself beyond contact,
as if I had no heart for pain;
now, she knows,
I've learned to be gentle.

She smirks as I button her clothes,
the last one hitting home
with the tasty click of a clean strike,
a smile that seems to me enigmatic
(and perhaps sceptical at the job I've done).
But in that smile,

I find a strain of love
I haven't known.

Sitting Room

Warm yourself –
the fire's picking up now.
I can place a glass of brandy in your hand,
if that's your thing.

There's nothing on the TV.
It jabbers like a senile uncle,
but it's nice to have it on, all the same.

Maybe you're the type
who likes a herbal tea –
a rooibos or a peppermint.
Maybe even a chamomile.

Am I right?

Such an array of moods I see:
giddy, tired, bitter, amused,
moments of sadness by the photographs.

And so many people:
friends and cousins,
little girls on laps,
teenagers who don't know where to stand,
chatty neighbours with crossed legs,
even the odd handyman.

But in the end, they all leave.

Wouldn't you like something?

Just tell me what I can get you.

Anything, anything at all.

Masquerade

Few things fascinate a child
more than brazen pretence.
They examine a reddened thumb
presented as a nose
or watch, bemused, a wordless adult
slurping absent tea.

It seems to them,
this world they've learned,
and all its laws of sight and touch,
have been discarded,
as if we can choose to take part
or fashion our own, secret realm.

But really, we're preparing them
to hone the art of mistrust,
teaching them to smell deceit
and forge through life
to safe domains,
to see adult faces as masks
twisted by experience.

We who've grown have learned
how to digest reality, daily,
drained of pretence
except in play.
And maybe, when we're jaded
with stillborn plans and busy days,
we need a court of make-believe
to pretend, for a while,

71

we're children ourselves.

Air-born

Time to taste
the power of wings,
the gusty physics of flight.

Courage crawls
from twigs and moss.
From a roof, your mother calls.

An eyeblink waltz:
no longer of land,
you're now a creature of air.

Bloated with momentum,
houses, trees and sudden walls
erupt from the placid background.

You feel the weight of descent
till you slap to ground,
tumble,
your vision blurred with shafts of grass.

There is another creature here,
with eyes that are greedy for you,
claws and fur
moving slow,
a mouth intent on showing you darkness.

Instinct beats your heart, your wings,
takes you up again,
but only as far as a window sill.

You're not quite there,
still unsure of this fluid terrain.

One hop
onto the air,
where wings speak a new language:
you join the society of birds.

Row 6

Our third plane trip together:
my daughter bends across her seat,
fascinated by fields below
in all their stained-glass shards
of brown, green and yellow.

A man in row 6
with black hair and grey streaks like thin cloud
watches us, and it seems to me,
his eyes are glazed in wistful thought,
as if he ponders another life:
sitting here where I am,
a daughter by his side.

I wonder if he remembers
a love that saw its end in talk
of children and their absence.
I want to tell him, *Don't regret*
that you won't suffer dark moods
from mangled sleep,
nights blent into bleary mornings
and watercolour weeks.

As if on cue,
my daughter works up to a gale of whining
over a broken pencil.
The food trolley approaches,
and I pay for a pleasant reprieve,
closing my eyes to savour it.

When they open, he's still there,
watching as she kisses me
and plucks her spoils from a bag of Maltesers.
Be happy with who you are, I tell him,
imagining myself in his seat:
row 6, by the window,
without anyone to attend to.

Room to Let

Coffee spoons?
No.
I've measured my life
in walls, fridges, balding couches,
houses shared like simmering saucepans
of routine, belief and ritual,
and often, questionable habits.

One guy I lived with,
Jean-Marc,
observed the custom
of washing his dishes once a week.
It took me a while,
but I did something to change his mind,
something you might consider extreme.

Over months and years,
I've gained friends and habits.
I've swum in the solitude of bedrooms,
each with its own personality
of shape,
smell
and view.
I've learned from others,
expanding my repertoire
of dinners speckled with rice and spices,
my knowledge of customs and cultures.

Lately, I've been using the word "mortgage",
so I'll need a new means

of measuring out my life.
Jean-Marc, wherever he is,
measured his week in sinkfuls.
A pity for him
it wasn't the odd plate or spoon:
he wouldn't have had to share his bed
with a medley of rice
and broken dishes.

Utility Room

I don't mean to bother you,
so I try to speak in a whisper.
What I mean is,
if you'd care to listen,
I don't see the need to raise my voice.
That's for others
who do it better.

I don't mind
that I'm undernourished,
like a child you forgot at the shop.
I've grown used to not being noticed.
In fact, I could even say
I quite like it now.

I wish, sometimes, I had more space,
but I have no say in the matter.
Whenever I do make noise,
I spasm with the spin of laundry
or dirty shoes slapped together.
It gives me terrible headaches, of course,
but I'm happy to be involved.

If I had a human name,
you might call me Frank,
wincing as the dog gets in
or when a pair of sweaty runners
are set down in the corner.

And let me share something with you:

it's actually quite funny
how perplexed men become
when a bulb they were sure was new
rattles softly to admit
it's now of no use.

The Hunt

In the bathroom, I dreamed of my daughter
as something other,
a starved beast that might hunt me from this room
if only she could smell me.

In recent months,
her teeth had broken through her gums
in readiness for the act;
she tired me
with cries at night that rattled my dreams away,
so I'd have no fight to give.

Her slow, light steps
stalked to the door.

I twisted the key,
submitted to her open arms,

the gentlest killing
I could ever imagine.

Cutting Grass

He steers the machine down the middle
to cleave the task in two,
knowing its busy rumble will signal
to neighbours and sheep he's at it again.

Forging toward the same corners,
overlapping and hoping
not to encounter a faint mohawk,
he whittles a sizeable patch to extinction.

Timid dips, a neighbourhood of moss –
he knows them all,
jabs doggedly at the flowerbed's edge,
tilts to the threat of a driveway kerb.

From the full-bellied bag,
a moist porridge of cuttings tumbles,
fruited pink with cherry blossom.
This light machine has new life
– and *he* does, determined to end
on the next load before it sags.

And when the job is done, silence.
A smell as if the earth itself is grateful.

Decay

Galway

By the fountain of Eyre Square
and the writhing flags of fourteen tribes,
you hear a woman warn of sin.
Soon, you feel the slope of Shop Street,
umbrellas held at sides,
where sallow-skinned ladies hug Oscar Wilde.

Imagine how it looked
hundreds of years before,
a medieval town of noise,
creaking carts full of food
and words you might not understand.
Some of those words endure.

The rain then was no worse,
and in this town, it's a constant theme
to enchant a rambling mind.
You watch the clouds bruise to a colour
that makes you look for shelter,
and still, you wish the sky would spare you,
would let you savour a simple walk,
but this sky is rarely so kind.

It's easy to ignore the cars
before you cross to Quay Street,
but not those thoughts
of eyeing shelves in Charlie Byrne's,
where a minute's search is hours lost.
You overhear the talk of books
from pinted folk on Neachtains chairs,

hearing the river's mumbled prayer,
as if asking forgiveness
for all the stray bodies it ensnared.

With a glance to the Spanish Arch,
you face the current, button your coat
and pass the garden at Jurys.
Further down, apartments are gathered
around what seems like a private pool,
and you imagine passers-by
thinking how it would be to live here,
watching the cool, still water
sucked down to the rushing river
in Guinnessy gusts of brown and white
that soon slip from view.

On along the leafy path,
you cross the road to wooden planks
that make a fool of those who rush
when rain has slickened its slant.
The river's company ends,
so you stop at the Salmon Weir Bridge.
A van waits before the bend,
where the turn of the bus is melodramatic.
When will they widen this bridge? you wonder,
stepping briefly onto the road,
your hair brushed by the bus's mirror
as Galway Cathedral faces you,
stout and grey, like an ageing queen
in a turquoise crown beaten plain
by decades of wintry rain.

Along the canal,
students stream en masse,
and you may recall with affection
years of essays, a girl in your class.
At Presentation Road,
something below the water shines;
you lean close to see it better –
like a red wound on dark stone:
a bottle of Buckfast wine.
The chunky, weathered wood of the sluice
restrains the charge of plastic and slime,
while frothy water seeps through,
dropping to a lower depth
a little at a time.

On Dominick Street, you glimpse a sculpture
behind a smudged window,
but you'll forget it by Raven Terrace,
crossing to the Claddagh
before it surrenders the Corrib to sea,
where a man engulfed in a blizzard of wings
throws bread discriminately.

Be careful as you step
round iron rings where dirty ropes
are tied to lilting boats.
A crow watches from a crossbar
two spaniels running between the posts.

A distant train leaves gingerly,
almost reluctant, it seems,
its many faces bound

for Dublin or some other place,
and you feel a stinging breeze
as winter descends on this town.
Then, a tap on your head
confirms the fear you had all along:
there isn't a crumb of shelter near
as rain comes lashing down.

Bin Day

One neighbour forgets
until she hears the measured yawn of crushed
     rubbish.
She rushes her bin to the road,
bed-warm still in her morning robe,
watches the upturned mess
taken like fish in one gulp.

Someone's bin has spilled its guts
to the wrath of a sudden gust.
It lies flat across the path,
courts the eyes of eager birds.
Another, however, looks more sedate,
a rock set on top, quite like a hat.

All have a vaguely coffin-ish form,
carrying off the weekly past,
with contents destined for mounds;
and as the road tightens
to the whims of cars parked askew,
behind the machine, a cortège forms
of those who'll be late for work.

Men with hardened faces
rush and shout through the blizzard of noise.
They must say the same things,
must hold a language of looks and signs.
Their clamour dissolves into the distance,
but they'll be back
to bury another week.

Terra Firma

Stop!

Do not trespass.

Fences, walls, gates and hedges
declare the owner's right
to claim this chunk of earth:
a territory compressed,
where rivers run at the turn of a wrist
and thin walls separate
food, faeces and breathy sex.

Have you ever stopped at a garden
and wondered what was there
before diggers and builders came?
Have you pondered
why hills and fields should be earned,
but not rain or air?

Stone, concrete and glass
rise from the ground
to occupy it with flagrant intention,
but all the numbers on doors,
all the signs you see on streets,
the lines on your map,
are a grand fiction.

Why not overthrow your neighbour,
fling your passport to the sea?
Open doors, lie in gardens,

because, after all,
land is free.

Rambla Nova, Tarragona

Here, where the blue air of a long September evening
is a warm soup of wandering
and distant ships with orange lights
are strips of street torn free from land,
my daughter holds my hand,
newly at ease with crowds,
me at ease with this foreign town.

Through the dark curtain of night,
we hear the waves
below the cliff on which we stand,
and she tells me we'll be there tomorrow,
flailing in the shallows,
churning up sand.

Unsaid

I

More than stone or wood,
silence
shapes a home,
imbeds itself
like damp in plaster.

Some fail
to turn out words
from the toil of their thoughts,
in fear of conflict
or naked nerves,

while others may devote years
to wordless war,
and this may bend
the air around them.

II

More than the absence of sound,
it's peace

and space,

a workshop to remake your mind
and all its spores of opportunity.

III

More than the clamour
of children, and all they pull from you,
the lasting lull of their departure
will take the wood of your voice
and strip it.

They'll return,
maybe with children of their own,
for just a dishevelled moment,
only to inhabit
the homes they've built themselves.

The final silence
is monstrous noise,
metal teeth devouring walls,
exposing powdery guts,
collapsing all to conceive a space
for new growth,
new silence,
new loves.

Small Goals

In Dunally, we worshipped sacred ground:
a garden skirted with fir trees
swaying like a sideline crowd.
We'd choose two teams,
careful to shape an equality of skill,
empty cans of gas for goalposts,
eyeing the size the others had given –
no goalie needed,
so stingy the gap.

One brother had balletic balance;
another had good positional sense;
the oldest would twist like a wind-up clock,
sensing the prospect of a bicycle kick
at the hint of a rising ball.

Neighbours came – David Clarke
was clinical, tidy;
Ultan Geraghty was hard in the tackle.
Dad leapt high for headers,
dealt advice and defended with arms
so wide the ball would strike his hand,
and we'd trot out the same old arguments.

Games went on till dark,
turning on the playroom light
to lend each moment a legible shape,
or we'd see our end
in Dad's drunken eyes –
sober, but in need of sugar

to cure his diabetic blood.

We've run to new patches of earth
– Galway, Dublin, Catalunya, Berlin –
and in the wrung minutes of a warm evening,
miles from the grass you once called home,
such memories are seeds,
and so you grow.

Bedroom

Always,
there is time for thought,
rippling over the floor, the walls,
while you perceive your life
as it is,
as it could be.

Don't obsess:
your bank balance,
the things people have said,
the lack of ambition in your meals,
none of these matter.

Think of the bed
as a thick cocoon to make you new
before the light stretches a hand
to stir you awake.

I will be here then too.

Always,
I will be your first and last,
the one to whisper,
"Good morning"
and "goodnight".

Adiós

Galway sheltered me – fourteen years;
now, it nudges me away
through morning cold,
with cracked hands on the bus to Shannon,
a sleeping child and a wife
wrapped in thought
at the hours ahead.

Nicole stirs in my arms
as the plane seeks communion with cloud,
breaking through like a fish leaping clear of the sea.
And when we land,
Tarragona is rich
with hills and voices, Roman stone
sprouting up from grass and walls
like spilt seeds of ancient ambition.

The wind is more Irish than we could've imagined,
so I pull the hood of Nicole's buggy
snug as a snail shell
and hold Sandra closer,
ignorant yet
of the months we'll spend without wifi or phone,
our rickety emotions,
the restless *cañas* and tapas.

From a footbridge, we smell the sea
and watch the wind provoke the waves
to foamy delirium.

Soon, the Mediterranean will calm,
cajoled to better humour by the sun,
and this city
will fill with new familiars.

Printed in Great Britain
by Amazon

44855290R00057